Around the Year With "The Cat at the Door"

About the authors

Louise Weldon is a hypnotherapist whose clients include children and adolescents who are working to improve their grades, behavior, and self-confidence. She also gives workshops on parenting skills and children's self-esteem. She is a former kindergarten teacher.

Anne Mather has been a professional writer for eighteen years. Her clients include the Task Force for Child Survival and Development and Emory University, among others. She has written extensively on addiction issues and is the author of *Bridging the Gap,* a guide for teenagers. She is a former middle- and high-school teacher.

Mather and Weldon coauthored *The Cat at the Door and Other Stories to Live By,* published by Hazelden Educational Materials.

Around the Year With "The Cat at the Door"

Affirmation Activities
For Ages Five and Older

Louise B. Weldon
Anne D. Mather

Hazelden Educational Materials
Center City, Minnesota 55012-0176

Library of Congress Cataloging-in-Publication Data
     Weldon, Louise B.
       Around the year with The cat at the door : affirmation activities for ages
    five and older / Louise B. Weldon, Anne D. Mather.
       p.   cm.
       "Adapted from Cat at the door"—CIP t.p. verso.
       ISBN 0-89486-937-X
       1. Creative activities and seatwork—Handbooks, manuals, etc. 2.
    Education, Elementary—Activity programs—Handbooks, manuals, etc. 3.
    Self-esteem in children—Handbooks, manuals, etc. I. Weldon, Louise B. II.
    Mather, Anne D. Cat at the door. III. Title.
    LB1027.25.M28 1993
    372.5—dc20   93-4590
                                                         CIP

Editor's note
    Hazelden Educational Materials offers a variety of information on chemical dependency and related areas. Our publications do not necessarily represent Hazelden's programs, nor do they officially speak for any Twelve Step organization.
    Permission to reprint the list on page 39 is granted by Dr. Jerry Coffey.

Acquisitions Editor: Vince Hyman
Design: David Spohn
Illustrations: Patrice Barton
Manuscript Editor: Caryn Pernu
Typesetter: Deborah Wischow
Copywriter: Alex Acker
Production Editor: Cindy Madsen
Print Manager: Joan Seim
Printer: Bang Printing
Type Style: Century Old Style and Avant Garde

Contents

Acknowledgments

We cannot name everyone whose enthusiastic support of *The Cat at the Door* has made it Hazelden's number-one kids' book. But we want to give special thanks to our moms, Millie Mather and Virginia Bishop, for being such great supporters. And all of the following bookstore and gift shop managers were, indeed, flag wavers and true promoters. We thank you.

Ruth Allen
Linda Bryant
Glenda Cannon
Marcia Duncan
Linda English
Rose-Mary Hatfield
Charlene Johnson
Rev. Ruth Ann LeBlanc
Rupert LeCraw
Rev. Denton O'Dell
Hilda McCarter
Carolyn McDaniel
Ray Majors
Carol Maxwell
Sandy Simons
Bill Thomas

Thanks also to the following people who helped kid-test these activities:

Matt Crews
Lois Edmond
Steve Epstein
Christopher Jenkins
Bill McBride
John Smith

Special thanks to Kris Mather for her class meeting concept.

We are also grateful to Hazelden's Vince Hyman and Caryn Pernu, our editors, and to Bobbie Rix and Leslie Johnson-Byrne for their support.

Introduction

Welcome to *Around the Year with "The Cat at the Door": Affirmation Activities for Ages Five and Older*.

As its name suggests, this manual offers a year's worth of weekly lesson plans for busy elementary school teachers, camp and guidance counselors, and youth directors of churches and synagogues. The activities in this workbook are also suitable for one-on-one sessions with youth counselors. All of these groups have helped boost *The Cat at the Door and Other Stories to Live By* to its position as Hazelden's number-one-selling children's book.

Both life skills development and values education are now a critical (and in some states, legislated) part of elementary school curricula. *The Cat at the Door* and this workbook are designed to address both. Each teaches stress-reducing and self-affirming life skills, such as positive self-talk, creativity, use of affirmations, and feeling identification. Each book also explores values, such as gratitude, honesty, forgiveness, and thoughtfulness toward others. The plans and activities are also designed to complement the three main styles of learning—kinesthetic, auditory, and visual—to appeal to all of your students.

But that sounds like teacher talk. In kids' language, this means they explore stories about their lives: handling a teaser, saying no, and dealing with a friend's unkind remark. As many teachers and counselors have attested, simply reading and discussing a story a day from *The Cat at the Door* with your students (there is one story for every day of the school year) can be a wonderful experience for your students while subtly introducing life-coping skills.

The manual adds more fun and structure. To kids, it means creativity mobiles, spider bulletin boards, and decoding secret messages. It means autograph books, hand puppets, and friendship booklets. It means homemade thank-you cards and gratitude garlands.

And it means games—usually noncompetitive—such as Affirmation Tic-Tac-Toe (page 10); a version of Go Fish in which kids fish for good thoughts (page 50); and the Happiness Game, in which children learn one another's unique preferences (page 32).

To facilitate these activities, twenty-five handouts and worksheets are included for photocopying. Also included are detailed descriptions of materials needed, preparation and pre-activities, discussion questions, and the activities themselves.

Incidentally, some activities require very little preparation. One is the first entry in the book, "Class Meeting," which details a simple but powerful teaching technique that can be used each week. There is also the "Celebration Certificate," a presentation of diploma-styled certificates for each child. The certificates say, in part: "This is to certify that a special event occurred on [date]. A marvelous child was born." In this case, the teacher need only fill in a child's birth date and name, but we guarantee it will be a moment that the children will treasure. (Author Louise Weldon usually presents all celebration certificates in one ceremony during the year. The children dress up for the occasion and take the event so seriously that one could hear a pin drop. And not incidentally, parents love the certificate too!)

Both of us are former teachers—Louise Weldon in kindergarten and Anne Mather in middle school and high school—and we are still active in teaching in youth programs. In addition, Louise recently coauthored a script for a TV pilot, a children's musical cartoon show designed to raise self-esteem.

You'll find these plans and activities have the ring of truth—indeed, most have been field-tested with our classes. (*The Cat at the Door* was also kid-tested; many educators feel that that is one reason the book is so appealing to children.)

Finally, we invite teachers, counselors, and all who work with children to send us feedback and other suggestions for using *The Cat at the Door* with children. Good luck! We hope you have as much fun using these activities as we had developing them.

Class Meeting

Materials:

- A copy of *The Cat at the Door*

Activity: Hold a twenty- to thirty-minute meeting each week, on the same day and at the same time. Gather in a circle with the children. Begin the discussion by explaining that the purpose of this weekly class meeting is problem solving. Explain that this is what adults do when they have a problem to tackle and that the skills the children learn here can be used in meetings throughout their lives.

Explain the terms *meeting* (a gathering of people to talk about and solve problems), *solutions* (answers to problems), *leader* (the person who sets the rules), and *brain-storming* (playing ideas off each other).

As the teacher, you are the leader and you go first. Read a selection from *The Cat at the Door* that applies to some behavior you've noticed recently in the classroom or playground, or heard the children discussing. Favorites include "Handling a Teaser," page 23; "Bus Trouble," page 124; "Asking for What You Want," page 71; "Your Secret Longing," page 63; and "The Worry-Free Way," page 58.

Follow with a brief discussion. Ask, *Has this ever happened to you? How did it make you feel? What solutions could you offer? What did you think of the solutions in the book?*

Invite individual children to share a problem, explaining that they must raise their hands to share a problem or to offer a solution. Stay out of the children's discussion at this point, except to refocus any child who wanders off into storytelling. Call on children for suggested solutions. After a child has received several possible suggestions for solving his or her problem, ask the child to report back at the beginning of the next meeting to tell the rest of the class what happened and what worked. Attention then turns to the next child with a problem to share. Each time you meet, four or five children can air their problems.

Variation: Occasionally, you can serve as a role model by reporting a problem you're having. ("I've been invited to two Christmas parties the same night; I don't know what to do.") Take several suggestions for solutions from the children, and report back at the beginning of the next week what you did and what solutions worked.

Editorial Note: Special thanks to Mrs. Kris Mather of Centerville Elementary School in Snellville, Georgia, who developed this class meeting concept based around our book. She reports that the weekly meeting is avidly anticipated by the children, who grapple with some real problems. Most important, she says, is that it gives the children confidence that they can do something about problems. Her meeting concept has been observed by counselors, other teachers, and administrators.

Thinking Small

Materials:

- Colored index cards, lined on at least one side
- Pencils

Pre-activity: Read "Think Small" (*The Cat at the Door,* page 62) and "Project Breakdown" (*The Cat at the Door,* page 132). Lead a discussion based on the following questions:

1. What do these stories have in common?
2. Both children feel overwhelmed. What do they do or realize that makes them stop feeling that way?

Activity: Pass out an index card to each child. Ask the children to list on the blank side a dream or wish that they have that seems unobtainable, or a project they can imagine facing (or really are facing) that seems so large they don't know how to tackle it. The children are not to sign the cards or give any indication of who wrote each card.

Collect the cards. Shuffle, and hand out the cards randomly to the students. Give the children five or ten minutes to study the cards, turn them over to the lined side, and list the steps that could help someone realize that goal or finish that project.

Collect the cards, and read the problems aloud in random order. Ask the class to vote on which problems to read the solutions to. Read several problems and their solutions. Always ask the children if they can think of any other steps or solutions not listed.

At the end of class, place the cards problem side up on the teacher's desk, so children can obtain the card they wrote if they're interested in the suggestions other students had for them.

Variation: For students in the lower elementary grades, you may select the unobtainable wish or dream. Then as a class or in small cooperative groups, students generate a list of steps to accomplish the task. If cooperative groups are used, ask each group to share its steps with the class.

Making Raps

Materials:

- Tape recorder
- Rap tape suitable for young children*
- Paper and pens or pencils

Pre-activity: This is another variation on "thinking small," based on the stories "Think Small" (*The Cat at the Door,* page 62) and "Project Breakdown" (*The Cat at the Door,* page 132). Read these two stories aloud to the class.

Activity: Play a rap song for the class. (Or announce your intentions the day before and ask the children to bring in their favorites.) Divide the class into small groups, and ask them to create their own raps. Rules for the raps are as follows:

1. They must clearly state a problem.
2. They must contain positive solutions.

Anything else can be thrown in—refrains, nonsense talk, whatever. Give the children plenty of time in class to work this out. Suggest that one student in each group write down what is agreed on. You may allow several days for this project, including time to practice—perhaps out on the playground or in the gymnasium or auditorium, with an aide in attendance.

Example:

I was feeling real shy.
Life was passing me by.
I couldn't even seem to say "Hi."
    You know what I mean.
    You know what I mean.

I talked to my bro'
For that's what he's for.
He helps me to grow and he helps me to soar.
    You know what I mean.
    You know what I mean.

*Several suggestions:** Cole's "Nursery Raps Starring Mother Goose" from MGM; "Rhythm, Rhyme, and Read Phonics" and "Rap with the Facts" by Twin Sisters Productions; "Phonics by Rock 'n Learn" by Rock 'n Learn; "Learning Wrap-Up" by Learning Wrap-Ups (for math only). All of these are available from teacher supply stores.

Making Bookmarks

Materials:

- Tagboard bookmarks
- Felt-tip pens or crayons

Preparation: Cut enough bookmarks (approximately 2 by 7 inches each) for the entire class, plus extras for mistakes. If students are going to use the bookmarks as gifts, cut several for each student.

Pre-activity: Read, or have a child read, "The World of Books" (*The Cat at the Door,* page 155).

Activity: Select—or ask students to choose—some favorite positive thoughts from *The Cat at the Door.* (A list of some is attached.) Or encourage the children to create their own positive thoughts based on the positive actions of their favorite book characters. Instruct the children to write their favorite affirmations on their bookmarks and to color them.

Encourage the children to use their bookmarks and to read their positive thoughts often when using their bookmarks.

Some short positive thoughts suitable for bookmarks

- I'm smart at being me.
- I'm special.
- I have a right to say no.
- I'm proud of myself.
- I'm happy.
- I like doing things for myself.
- I feel good.
- I can control my worrying.
- I can make my dreams happen.
- I like my family.
- When I think I can, I can!
- I'm happy from the inside out.
- I enjoy sharing.
- I'm honest.
- I know I am wonderful.
- I make good decisions.
- I like being me.
- I can say what I want and don't want.

Affirmation Stickers

Materials:

- Box of self-adhesive copier labels, printer labels, typewriter address labels, or self-adhesive badges. Try to have one page of labels for each child. For children in lower grades who need more space to write, substitute index cards, which can be taped or pinned to clothing.
- Felt-tip markers

Pre-activity: Read "Mind Grooming" (*The Cat at the Door,* page 165) to the children, or ask one of them to read it. Point out that Mrs. Barton says nice things to herself to build herself up. Teach the children the term *affirmation* and the key concepts behind affirmations:

- Affirmations are positive thoughts.
- They usually start with an "I" statement. (Mrs. Barton's is "I am sure I will give a good talk.")
- When we repeat them often, we feel better about ourselves.

Activity 1: If you have several copies of *The Cat at the Door,* let each child flip through the book and choose his or her favorite positive thoughts, which are in bold face at the bottom of each story. Ask the children to copy the affirmations they choose onto address labels or badges and then color them. The labels can be peeled off and put on notebooks, schoolbags, or clothing.

Activity 2: Ask the children to create their own affirmations and write them on their labels. Encourage the children to keep their affirmations simple, like the following:

- *I am happy.*
- *I am a worry-free kid.*
- *I am open about my feelings.*

Ideally, the children should each get a whole sheet of labels to create affirmations as they need them. For example, if over a weekend they start feeling nervous about making friends, they can create an affirmation to combat these negative thoughts, such as "I am friendly and attract good friends."

Affirmation Relay

Materials:

- Index cards with affirmations written on them
- Two chairs

Preparation: Copy positive thought affirmations from *The Cat at the Door* onto separate index cards.

Pre-activity: Read "The Positive-Thinking Habit" (*The Cat at the Door,* page 157) to the class, or ask one of the children to read it. Have a brief discussion based on the following questions:

1. What does Don say to Melissa about "positive thought stuff"?
2. What do you think Don means by "positive thought stuff"?
3. What habit is Don trying to change?
4. Do you have a habit you would like to change?
5. Why does it take some time for Don to change his habit?

Activity: To play the affirmation relay game, ask the children to form two lines in the back of the room. Place two chairs in the front of the room, and put a pile of index cards with affirmations written on them on each chair. When you say "Go," the first student in each line runs up to the chair and picks up an affirmation card. Both stand behind their chairs and read the affirmations out loud so their teammates can hear them. Then they pick up another card and run it to the next student in line, who runs behind the chair and reads the new affirmation out loud. The line that finishes first wins.

After the game is over, pass the affirmation cards out to the class. Ask the students to tell how they can use their affirmations in real-life situations or to name real people who are living examples of these ideas.

Affirmation Tic-Tac-Toe

Materials:

- Masking tape
- Nine index cards per game
- Tic-tac-toe sentences (page 11)

Preparation: Make a 6-by-6-foot tic-tac-toe board on the floor using masking tape. Prepare nine index cards by writing "Yes" on one side and "No" on the reverse side of each card. Photocopy page 11, and cut the copy into separate sentence strips.

Pre-activity: Read "I Don't Put Myself Down" (*The Cat at the Door,* page 35) to the children, or ask one of the children to read it out loud. Have a brief discussion focused on the following questions:

1. What does Alex say to himself, or to others, that puts himself down?
2. What unkind words do people you know say about themselves?
3. What does it mean to say "My words can be my best friends or my worst enemies"?
4. Describe some ways you can be a good friend to yourself.

Activity: Ask the students to line up at the tic-tac-toe board. Give a sentence strip to the first child to read. (Read the sentence for the child if he or she can't read.) Ask, "Is that something good to say to yourself?" Give the student a "Yes" or a "No" card according to his or her answer. The student then chooses a place to stand on the tic-tac-toe board. (Yes = O and No = X) The game continues until a line of three Yeses or Noes in a row is formed.

If the Noes form the first line, ask the children with the No cards to think of a way to change the sentences on their strips into positive sentences. Then the children with the No cards can turn their cards over to Yes so that positive sentences form the three in a row.

Editorial Note: This is a noncompetitive game. Several games can be played concurrently by selecting team captains to hand out the Yes and No cards and sentence strips, and by creating more game areas.

Affirmation Sentences for Tic-Tac-Toe

I love myself.

I am friendly.

I enjoy having fun.

I can always find a solution to my problems.

I like myself.

I can never get along with my sister.

I feel stupid.

I am so dumb. I can't learn math.

I hate it when I make mistakes.

Nobody likes me.

I am a good friend.

I can do it.

I treat myself very well.

I am proud of things I do.

I'm just a blabbermouth.

I don't make friends easily.

Boxcar Brags

Materials:

- Pattern for train engine and boxcars (pages 13-14)
- Markers or crayons
- Tape or thumbtacks

Preparation: Photocopy a boxcar for each child in the class; the engine is for the teacher.

Pre-activity: Read "I Think I Can!" (*The Cat at the Door,* page 91) to the children, or ask one of them to read it out loud. Have a brief discussion based on the following questions:

1. Ever since Brent was a little boy he has been taught the power of positive thinking. What do you think the phrase "the power of positive thinking" means?
2. Why do you think the story "The Little Engine That Could" is Brent's favorite?
3. How can our thinking help us learn new activities like riding a larger bicycle, playing a new sport, or learning to dance?
4. What is something new you have learned to do this year?

Activity: Give out boxcar handouts. Ask the children to sign their name on their boxcar. Then ask them to color the boxcars, completing the phrase "I can . . ." with one thing they can do. (Examples: *I can read. I can write my name. I can sing.*)

On the train engine, write your name and an "I can" affirmation. Collect the boxcars and assemble the train as a bulletin board or as a class display in the hallway.

Follow-up: The next day, read "Positive Talk and Pictures" (*The Cat at the Door,* page 74). Discuss these questions:

1. How does Jerry help himself learn to skateboard?
2. What does Alice do to help herself learn to ride a bicycle?
3. What are some ways you can use your mind to help you learn new things?

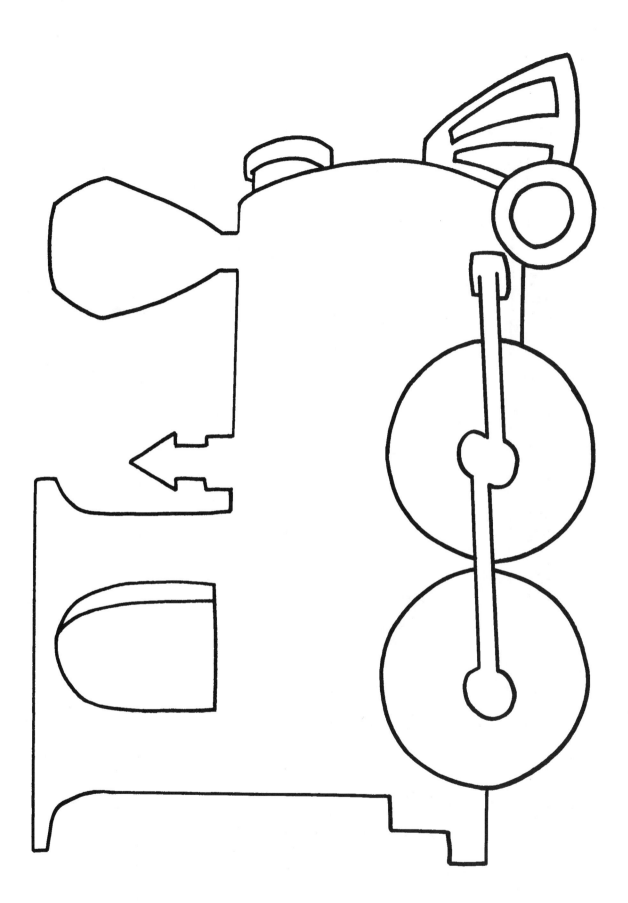

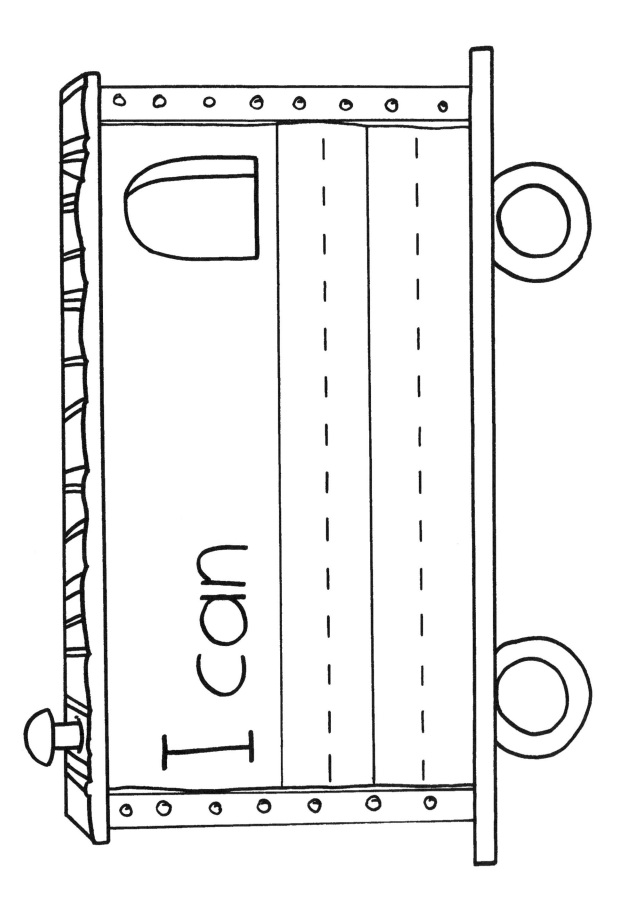

I can

The Balloon Express

Materials:

- A copy of the balloon and basket pattern (page xx) for each child
- Colored yarn or ribbon
- Strips of white paper
- Markers or crayons
- Pencils
- Glue

Preparation: Make a copy of the balloon handout for each child in the class. Cut out enough 2-inch strips of white paper for each child to have two.

Pre-activity: Read "The Balloon Express" (*The Cat at the Door,* page 159), or ask one of the children to read the story to the class. Have a brief discussion based on the following questions:

1. What are some things that have happened in your life that have made you so mad or sad that you felt like crying?
2. What does Erica do to help let her feelings out?
3. What are some things you can do when you feel sad or mad to help yourself express your feelings? (List the students' responses on the blackboard.)
4. Do you have a choice as to how you express your feelings?

Activity: Give each child a piece of construction paper, a balloon handout, and two strips of white paper. Ask the children to color the balloon and make a poster by gluing the sail of the balloon to the top half of the construction paper and gluing the basket to the bottom of the page. Tell the children to put glue only on the sides and bottom of the basket so that it forms a pocket, and then to attach the sail to the basket with two pieces of yarn. Pass out strips of white paper and ask the students to write down any hurt feelings or angry feelings that they are ready to let go of. Tell them to fold the strips so that the writing doesn't show, and to glue the strips into the basket.

After the children are finished making their baskets, ask them to imagine that their balloons are flying up and up and taking away their hurt and angry feelings.

Color and cut out the balloon and the basket. Glue the balloon and basket on construction paper, and attach the balloon to the basket with yarn. Leave the top of the basket unglued.

Celebration Certificate

Materials:

- A copy of the Celebration Certificate (page 18) for each child in class
- Fine felt-tip pen

Preparation: Fill out a certificate for each child in class. (Certificates look nicer if they are copied on parchment.)

Pre-activity: Read "A Personal Celebration" (*The Cat at the Door,* page 84) to the class, or ask a student to read it. Have a brief discussion based on the following questions:

1. Name some things people do to celebrate the Fourth of July at Lake Burton.
2. In the story, how does Andy celebrate this holiday?
3. Tell about another day you celebrate.

Activity: Create a ceremony in which you present a certificate to each student.

Certificate

This is to certify that a special event occurred on

_____.

A marvelous child was born.

This child, named _____, is a great child

and is made of love and joy and all things wonderful.

This child is smart and creative.

My Autograph Book

Materials:

- A copy of the autograph book handout (page 20) for each child
- Construction paper or Fun Foam (thin, colored foam rubber, available in large sheets from craft stores) for cover
- Pens, crayons, or pencils
- Stapler

Preparation: Photocopy enough handouts for each student in the class. Make enough covers for the autograph books. (They should be the size of one page on the handout.) Use either construction paper or Fun Foam for the covers.

Pre-activity: Read "Different Kinds of Genius" (*The Cat at the Door,* page 77). Lead a discussion, asking the children what qualities they like in friends. Ask the children to come to the board and write down the qualities (interested in others, enthusiastic, fun, a good listener). Or break the class into cooperative groups to discuss and list the qualities they like in friends.

Activity: Pass out autograph handouts and book covers. Ask children to cut out the pages and staple them together, placing the cover on top. On the cover, they should write their name and "My Autograph Book." Once they have assembled their books, children are to get autographs of people who have qualities they admire. Urge the children to keep their books in a private place to read when they're feeling lonely or unhappy.

Variation: Write the following rhymes on the board. Ask children to copy one onto the first page of their autograph books.

This is my autograph book.
I look at it when I'm blue.
Please sign your name
And something nice too.

People are geniuses at many things:
Being kind, funny, or just "true blue."
I keep this book as a reminder
That I feel this way about you.

Creativity Mobile

Materials:

- Mobile pattern (page 22) copied on card stock for each child (This requires a special copier, available at copying stores.)
- Markers or crayons
- Pencils
- Scissors
- Hole puncher
- Yarn
- Stapler

Pre-activity: Read "'Paws' For Creativity" (*The Cat at the Door,* page 133) to the class, or ask one of the children to read it. Discuss the following questions:

1. What is the theme for Jeremy's creative writing class?
2. What are some other things that children can create?
3. What are two meanings of the phrase "'Paws' for Creativity"?
4. Do you have creative ideas? What can you do to get more creative ideas?
5. What are some affirmations that you could say to yourself about creativity? (Examples: *I am creative. I have lots of creative ideas. I have creative thoughts. Everyone has creativity. I like to create fun things. Creativity is fun.*)

Activity: Give each child a pattern for the creativity mobile. Give the children the following directions: Write an affirmation about creativity on each pattern piece and then decorate each piece. Cut out the pieces, and punch a hole in the top of each piece. Punch five holes about an inch apart in the long strip. Make a circle with the strip and staple the ends together. Attach the pattern pieces to the long strip by threading the yarn through the hole in each piece and through a hole in the strip. Knot both ends. Punch two more holes opposite each other on the strip and string a 12-inch piece of yarn through the holes. Knot both ends and hang the mobile.

I AM CREATIVE!

Decoding a Secret

Materials:

- Pencils
- Handout for decoding a secret (page 24)

Pre-activity: Read "Word Watch" (*The Cat at the Door,* page 33) to the children, or ask one of them to read the story out loud. Have a brief discussion based on the following questions:

1. Describe how Joel feels when his dad tells him they need to get new shoes before soccer practice.
2. What word does Joel learn from his brother Dave that describes how he's feeling?
3. What does *overwhelm* mean?
4. Describe a time when you felt overwhelmed. What did you do about it?

Activity: Use the symbols on the chart to decode the secret affirmations. Each set of two symbols stands for a letter of the alphabet. Find the first symbol down the left-hand column and find the second symbol across the top column. The mystery letter is revealed where the two columns intersect. For example, the letter **I** is represented by |**X**.

Variation: For variety, each child can also choose an affirmation to encode using the code chart, and then exchange the new puzzle with a classmate and decode each other's affirmations.

Editorial Note: This activity also reinforces graph reading and may coordinate with children's math studies.

Decoding a Secret

Directions: To decode the secret affirmation, find the first symbol in the column on the left and the second symbol across the top column. The mystery letter is where the symbols meet.

	Σ	■	⊥	X	Θ
−	A	B	C	D	E
|	F	G	H	I	J
O	K	L	M	N	O
Δ	P	Q	R	S	T
≡	U	V	W	X	Y

■O Θ− Θ− Σ| X| ⊥≡ ΘO ⊥|

Θ≡ Σ− XΔ ΘO ΘΘ XΔ X− XΔ Θ≡ ⊥O XΔ X− XΘ X| Σ|

XΘ ■ XΘ XΘ Σ| ■ ΘO ⊥| Δ≡ ΘO ⊥≡ XΔ XΔ Θ− ⊥Δ X≡ Θ− X|

Intelligent Spider Bulletin Board

Materials:

- A copy of the spider handout (page 26) for each child
- Large yarn or construction paper spider web (may be bought from a craft store)
- Two-sided tape, UHU Holdit plastic adhesive, or push-pin tacks
- Crayons

Pre-activity: Read "An Intelligent Place to Live" (*The Cat at the Door*, page 104) to the children, or have one of them read it to the class. Have a brief discussion, focusing on the following questions:

1. Do you have a pet? Do you think your pet is intelligent? Why?
2. Have you ever noticed a spider web? What does it look like? Do you agree with John that such complex beauty shows intelligence? Do you think you could make a spider web overnight?
3. What other animals or insects do you think of as intelligent?
4. John decides that not only animals but also plants and "everything" have intelligence. What things around you do you think show intelligence? (Examples: the solar system, the stars, flowers budding.)
5. People usually use the term *intelligence* to mean being smart at learning in school. But this story shows that intelligence is also "know-how." In what areas, besides school, can people have a natural "know-how"? (Lead discussion into such areas as sports, crafts, listening, and being a good friend.)

Activity: Point out the spider web on the bulletin board. Ask the children to write or draw something that they have "know-how" about on the belly of the spider on their handouts, and sign their name. Then they may color the spider. When their handouts are completed, the students pin or stick their spiders onto the web. Give children time to read what others have written.

Variation: Students may cut out the spider body and use pipe cleaners for legs.

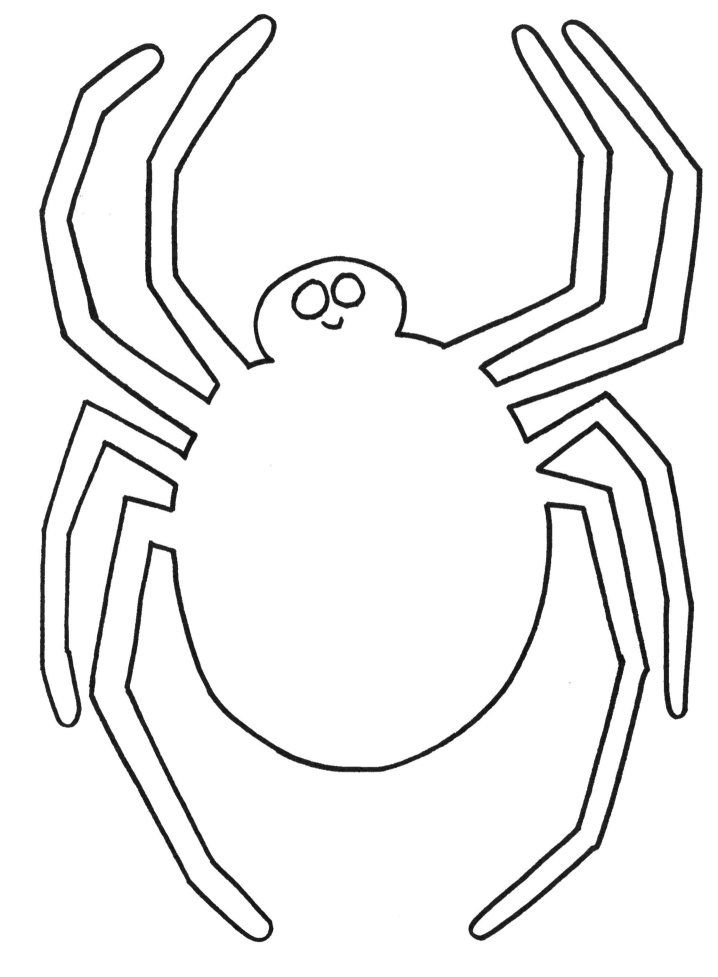

Jumpin' It Out—I

Pre-activity: Read the story "Jumpin' It Out" (*The Cat at the Door,* page 127) to the class, or ask a child to read it out loud. Teach the children the following rhyme:

Jump up and down.
Jump all about.
It's a good way
To let anger out.

Activity: On the playground or in the gym, ask the children to form a big circle. One by one, the children say something that really makes them mad. After each statement, all the children respond in unison by chanting the rhyme while they jump up and down.

Throw some body language variation into this, like for doing the Hokey-Pokey: shaking parts of the body, turning around, and so on. Teachers can also make this more fun by encouraging the children to groan, moan, or otherwise vocalize their agreement with a situation that makes another child mad, before launching into the rhyme.

Variation: For quiet times, children can hug a teddy bear or other stuffed animal. Teach them the rhyme:

Hug my teddy bear.
Hug teddy tight.
It's a good way
To set anger right.

Jumpin' It Out—II

Materials:

- Paper
- Pencils

Pre-activity: Read "Jumpin' It Out" (*The Cat at the Door,* page 127) to the children, or ask one of them to read it to the class. Have a brief discussion based on the following questions:

1. How did Alex feel when his parents got divorced?
2. How does Alex show his anger at school?
3. What does Alex learn from his school counselor about new ways to express angry feelings?
4. What are some things you get angry about?
5. How can we let our anger out without hurting ourselves or someone else? *Examples:*
   - Say you are angry: *I am angry. I am upset. I am really mad at you.*
   - Write an angry note to the person you are mad at and then tear the note up.
   - Walk away and cool off.
   - Talk to a friend about your upset feelings.
   - Do some kind of physical exercise.

Activity: Ask the children to make up a rhyme, a poem, or a rap about expressing angry feelings without hurting anyone.

Example:

When I feel angry,
I don't hit or yell.
I talk about my feelings.
I find a friend to tell.

Children read their poems to the class after they finish them.

Picture Perfect

Materials:

- A copy of the picture frame handout (page 30) for each child
- Crayons and pencils
- Yarn
- Construction paper
- Buttons

Pre-activity: Read "I'm Smart At Being Me" (*The Cat at the Door,* page 1) to the children, or ask one of them to read it to the class. Discuss the following questions:

1. What does Jimmy spend a lot of time doing at the beginning of the story?
2. What are some things Jimmy's friends like about him?
3. What does it mean to be smart at being yourself?
4. Name some ways you are smart at being you.

Activity: Give each child a copy of the picture frame handout. Ask the children to draw a picture of themselves. They may use yarn, construction paper, or buttons for hair, eyes, or other features.

I'm a wonderful child;
That's easy to see.
I'm always smart
At being me.

Solution Brainstorm Session

Materials:

- Index cards
- Watch or timer
- Pens or pencils

Pre-activity: Read to the children, or have one of them read aloud, "More Solutions Than You Can Dream Of" (*The Cat at the Door,* page 70). Explain that if we just think about a problem, we often surprise ourselves with the answers we can come up with. To prove this, the class is going to play a game.

Activity: Choose four volunteers: two to be "recorders," one to be timekeeper, and one to dispense the cards as needed. Divide the rest of the class into two groups.

Hand each child a card, and tell the children to write down one problem situation. If any of the children seem to be having difficulty, prompt them by suggesting common problem areas, such as schoolwork, brothers and sisters, pets, friendships, or playing at recess.

Collect the cards from each group. Then give each group the other group's cards. The teams take turns brainstorming, with one person prompting his or her team in a timed period. Each student takes a turn reading a problem card. The group members call out all the solutions they can think of in one minute. The recorders write down the solutions. (It should take two to keep up with the activities.) When one minute passes, it is the other team's turn for a student to pick a card, read it aloud, and prompt for solutions.

The winning team is the one that comes up with the most solutions to all of the problems.

The Happiness Game

Materials:

- A game handout (page 33) for each child
- Pens
- Markers or crayons
- Buttons (to use as playing pieces)
- One die or game spinner for every two children

Pre-activity: Read the story, "An Inside Job" (*The Cat at the Door,* page 98). Have a brief discussion. Ask, *Rodney says swimming makes him happy. Do you like to swim? What activities make you happy?*

The discussion should lead toward the idea that different things make different people happy, and that's OK.

Activity: Distribute the game handouts. Tell the children to write or draw on each block something that makes them happy. Ask the children not to talk with one another about this because part of the fun is discovering our differences. The other part is discovering how many things there are in life that make us happy.

As a way to prompt children, tell them to imagine going through the day or week, remembering what they do at different times of the day. Give the children about ten minutes to fill in their blocks. Then ask them to color their games.

Ask each child to pair up with another and take turns playing each other's game to learn what makes that person happy. Hand out buttons or pennies, to be used as game pieces, and dice or spinners, which can be borrowed from another game. A turn consists of rolling the die (or spinning the spinner) and moving that number of spaces. The child then reads aloud what is on the block. The first person to the end "wins," but the point of the game is to remind ourselves how much we have to be happy about and to learn more about what makes someone else happy.

Editorial Note: This game is a good icebreaker in newly formed groups or classes. It may also provide an activity for pairs of children who finish their work early. Or during a counseling session, a counselor may play this game with a client.

Start

Finish!

Macaroni Magic

Materials:

- Box (at least shoe box size) with a slit in the top, covered with colored construction paper
- Two small bags of alphabet macaroni (found in the pasta or soup section of supermarkets)
- Glue
- Marker

Pre-activity: Read "Easy Answers" (*The Cat at the Door,* page 122). Talk briefly about solutions and the fact that others can sometimes easily see the answers to our problems—and vice versa.

Tell the children that the class is going to create a solution box, which will always be kept on the teacher's desk.

Activity: Using a large marker, write the words "Solution box for" on the box. Then tell the children to sift through the macaroni to find the letters in their name. They may then glue their macaroni name to the box. (Try to fit all the names on one side, preferably the front, so letters don't get knocked off.)

Explain how the solution box will work: Each week, a child suggests a puzzling situation or problem and writes it on the chalkboard. Children are to drop their suggestions for solving the situation in the solution box during the week. On Fridays, the teacher and students count and discuss the numerous solutions.

For the first week, illustrate the process by paraphrasing a story from *The Cat at the Door,* leaving out the solution. For example, you might write on the board: "trouble with a bully on the school bus." At the end of the week, after all the students' suggestions have been discussed, read "Bus Trouble" (*The Cat at the Door,* page 124) to the class.

How to Say No

Activity: Read aloud, or have a child read, "Learning to Say No" (*The Cat at the Door,* page 21). Lead a discussion with the children about questions they find hard to answer honestly. If discussion lags, some situations you might use as prompts include the following: others asking to borrow your clothes or games; doing something a friend wants you to do that you disagree with; dealing with a friend who asks to copy your homework.

Point out that the story gives a three-part formula for saying no. The three parts are as follows:

1. *I know* . . . (Let the person know you understand what he or she wants.)
2. *But* . . . (Simply and shortly say your feelings.)
3. *So* . . . (Say what you want or don't want.)

Write these three parts on the chalkboard, and list some of the problems the children talked about during the discussion. Urge the students to complete the sentences for their problems. For younger students, provide several complete *I know. . . But. . . So. . .* examples for them to follow.

Easy-Yes, Easy-No Circle Game

Pre-activity: Do the "How to Say No" exercise (page 35).

Activity: This is a fast-paced, short, deceptively easy game, in which students practice saying no. Ask the class to form a large circle. Stand in the middle of the circle and ask the students questions they suggested during earlier class discussions of saying no, questions that the children are uncomfortable saying no to.

All the children have to do, when a question is directed to them, is say "No."

Example:

> TEACHER [*facing Linda*]: Linda, may I borrow your Nintendo game today?
> LINDA: No.
> TEACHER [*elaborates, asking several times*]: Oh, please, I just want to borrow it today. I'll return it tomorrow, I promise.
> LINDA: No.
> TEACHER: Oh, come on. Just once. I'd do it for you.
> LINDA: No.

The point of this game is to get children comfortable saying no without explanation. Other children should be encouraged to clap after each child's response.

Making a Special Placemat

Purpose: This is a gratitude-building exercise, meant to help the children and their families realize how much they appreciate each other.

Materials:

- Plain or colored construction paper
- Crayons
- Laminator
- Note to parents

Preparation: Write a note to the parents explaining the purpose of their child's gift placemat. Photocopy the note to send home with each child.

Pre-activity: Read "The Special Plate" (*The Cat at the Door,* page 14). Lead a discussion about special things the children notice about their family members.

Activity: Pass out plain or colored construction paper. Ask children to design a special placemat for a member of their family, or one for the whole family to share. Make sure that the children sign their placemats.

Collect the placemats and laminate them. This makes a good—and unique—gift. When you return the placemats to the children, give each child a note to bring home.

Follow-up: About two weeks after this lesson, ask the children if their placemats have been used in their home and for what occasions.

Beating Boredom

Materials:

- Lined paper
- Handout of things to do (page 39)
- Blackboard or flip chart

Pre-activity: Read "The Boredom Cure" (*The Cat at the Door,* page 181). Ask the children, *When are you most often bored?* List these situations on the blackboard or flip chart.

Activity: Ask the children to start a numbered list of things to do when they are bored. Afterward, ask the children to read their lists and the number of activities they thought of.

Then combine the lists on the flip chart or blackboard. As a child thinks of an item not on the list, she or he can go up and add it. When the list is done, the teacher can make the list into a poster, titled creatively (for example, "The students in Classroom X have learned how to beat the boredom blues!") and hang it in the hall outside the classroom or in the classroom. Make photocopies of the list for the children to take home.

Editorial Note: This idea is the inspiration of a North Carolina child psychologist, Dr. Jerry Coffey. Dr. Coffey put a blank list at the receptionist's desk at his practice. Visitors were encouraged to add things to the list. Over eighty activities resulted! (See the list on page 39.) You may wish to hand out Dr. Coffey's list and see how it compares with the ideas your students came up with.

KIDS
Nothing to do today?

Take a walk
Play tennis
Go fishing
Go to a movie
Make a pie
Play basketball
Go tubing
Make a tape recording
Camp out
Make a paper airplane
Call your grandma
Start a garden
Go swimming
Write a letter
Jump rope
Play badminton
Draw a picture
Do hula hoop
Throw a ball
Write a poem
Rent a movie
Ride a bike
Go on a picnic
Play softball
Skip a rock
Call a friend
Play marbles
Try a yo-yo
Jump on an inner tube
Blow bubbles
Watercolor
Climb a tree
Make a sandbox
Do a sidewalk chalk drawing
Dance
Make a grass harp
Look at a globe
Explore with a magnifying glass
Make sock puppets
Raise a chicken
Pick wildflowers

Make some cookies
Go skating
Make a model
Play old maid
Play soccer
Get an ice cream cone
Ride a horse
Have a cookout
Visit a church
Make some stilts
Join scouts
Take a drive
Go to the park
Play red rover
Go bowling
Play gin rummy
Join 4-H
Bake a cake
Make popcorn balls
Play tag
Listen to music
See a ball game
Play checkers
Make ice cream
Play hide-and-seek
Go to a remote control raceway
Find a four-leaf clover
Start an ant farm
Make a rope swing
Look at baby pictures
Read a book
Take a hike
Sing
Read a map
Plan a vacation
Run a Kool-Aid stand
Have a treasure hunt
Wade in a creek
Go hiking
Bathe the dog

The Gratitude Garland

Materials:

- Sticky Strips or Sticky Shapes (gummed strips for making chains, available at craft stores) OR sheets of Fun Foam (thin, colored sheets of foam rubber available at craft stores), one 18-by-12-inch sheet for every two or three children, OR colored construction paper strips
- Staplers (small enough to fit the chain)
- Permanent markers
- Scissors

Preparation: Cut the Fun Foam or construction paper into 6-by-3/4-inch strips (forty-eight strips per sheet for Fun Foam, twenty-four for construction paper), or mark the sheets for the children to cut. (Sticky Strips and Sticky Shapes are precut.)

Pre-activity: Read "The Chain of Love" (*The Cat at the Door,* page 29).

Activity: Distribute several strips to each student, or pass out marked sheets for the children to cut into strips. Ask the children to list on the strips things they are thankful for, one item per strip. About ten minutes into the exercise, ask individual children to volunteer to read aloud what they have written. (The other students can continue writing while classmates are reading their lists.) This will enlighten others and be a catalyst for more ideas. Remind children to think small (microwave popcorn) as well as big (memories, nature, home).

There are several options for the chains:

1. Students write good things about their class, teacher, and school on strips of paper and connect the strips into a classroom chain. Children read their strips out loud as they connect their strips to the chain. (Sticky Strips self-connect when licked; others need to be stapled.) Make sure the words are on the outside of the garland. Children or the teacher can hang the gratitude garland somewhere in the classroom.

2. The students can make a personal "chain of love" to hang in their own rooms. Each child can write whatever he or she wants. In this case, children staple their own chains and do not read the strips out loud.

Feelings Word Find

Materials:

- A copy of the word find handout (page 42) for each child
- Pens or pencils

Pre-activity: Read "Word Watch" (*The Cat at the Door,* page 33). Hold a discussion about feelings. Some key points you may want to discuss include the following:

1. Everyone has feelings.
2. Having a name for a feeling helps you realize that that feeling is normal.
3. Others may not show their feelings the same way you do.

Activity: Hand out the "Feelings Word Find." Instruct the children to circle as many feelings or emotions as they can. Hidden words may run up, down, forward, backward, or diagonally in the puzzle.

Answer:

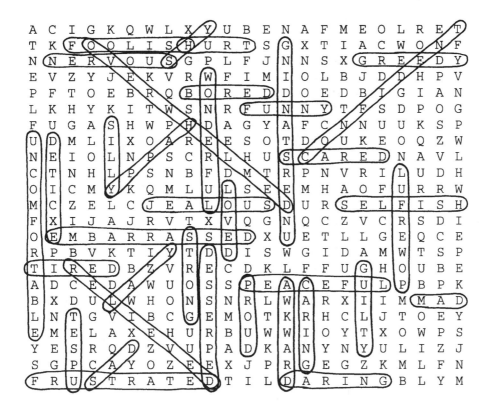

Feelings Word Find

```
A C I G K Q W L X Y U B E N A F M E O L R E T
T K F O O L I S H U R T S G X T I A C W O N F
N N E R V O U S G P L F J N N S X G R E E D Y
E V Z Y J E K V R W F I M I O L B J D D H P V
P F T O E B R Q B O R E D D O E D B I G I A N
L K H Y K I T W S N R F U N N Y T F S D P O G
F U G A S H W P H D A G Y A F C N N U U K S P
U D M L I X O A R E E S O T D O U K E O Q Z W
N E I O L N P S C R L H U S C A R E D N A V L
C T N H L P S N B F D M T R P N V R I L U D H
O I C M Y K Q M L U L S E E M H A O F U R R W
M C Z E L C J E A L O U S D U R S E L F I S H
F X I J A J R V T X V Q G N Q C Z V C R S D I
O E M B A R R A S S E D X U E T L L G E Q C E
R P B V K T I Y T D D I S W G I D A M W T S P
T I R E D B Z V R E C D K L F F U G H O U B E
A D C E D A W U O S S P E A C E F U L P B P K
B X D U L W H O N S N R L W A R X I I M M A D
L N T G V I B C G E M O T K R H C L J T O E Y
E M E L A X E H U R B U W W I O Y T X O W P S
Y E S R Q D Z V U P A D K A N Y N Y U L I Z J
S G P C A Y O Z E E X J P R G E G Z K M L F S
F R U S T R A T E D T I L D A R I N G B L Y M
```

Words Hidden in the Feelings Word Find

awkward
bored
caring
confident
daring
depressed
embarrassed
excited
foolish
frustrated
funny
greedy

guilty
happy
hurt
jealous
lazy
loved
mad
nervous
overwhelmed
peaceful
powerful
proud

relieved
sad
scared
selfish
shy
silly
strong
tired
uncomfortable
understanding
upset
wonderful

Sharing Feelings

Materials:

- A copy of the feeling strips handout (page 44)
- Scissors
- A lunch bag
- Markers

Preparation: Decorate the lunch bag with a face that expresses a strong emotion. Draw the face so that the hair is at the open end of the bag. Cut out the feeling word slips and put them in the bag.

Pre-activity: Read "Sharing Feelings" (*The Cat at the Door,* page 78) to the children, or ask one of them to read it. Discuss the following questions:

1. What does Frank talk to his troop leader about?
2. Mr. Abbott tells Frank something he learned about giving love. What is it?
3. How had Frank been handling his feelings before his talk with Mr. Abbott?
4. What are the ways Mr. Abbott helps Frank?

Talk about some ways that people express feelings: showing feelings in their facial expressions, saying what they are feeling, and acting out what they are feeling. Ask the children to share ways that they show their feelings.

Activity: Each child draws a feeling slip out of the bag you have prepared and takes a turn pantomiming the expression of that feeling. Children can use gestures and facial expressions or act it out.

Feeling Strips

Happy	Embarrassed
Sad	Nervous
Angry	Content
Afraid	Resentful
Lonely	Glad
Bored	Disappointed
Confused	Anxious
Frustrated	Defeated
Humiliated	Silly
Mad	Wild card: Child chooses feeling to express.
Confident	Wild card: Child chooses feeling to express.

Feeling Pictures

Materials:

- A copy of the feeling pictures handout (page 46) for each student
- Markers or crayons

Pre-activity: Read "The New Pen" (*The Cat at the Door,* page 25) to the children, or ask one of them to read it. Discuss the following questions:

1. What has made Molly uncomfortable?
2. Is it a good idea to do things just to please other people?
3. What questions does Cathy suggest Molly ask herself when she feels hesitant about making a decision?
4. What lesson does Molly learn from giving her pen away?

Activity: Give each student a copy of the feeling pictures handout. Ask students to draw pictures that represent each feeling beside the feeling words. They may draw things that might cause the feeling, a picture of someone who is experiencing that feeling, or an abstract representation of that feeling.

Feeling Pictures

Directions: Draw pictures that represent the feeling words listed below.

Angry	Frustrated
Bored	Lonely
Confused	Silly
Disappointed	Happy
Embarrassed	Scared

Good-Bye to Worry

Materials:

- White construction paper
- Pencils

Pre-activity: Read "The Worrywart's Pledge" (*The Cat at the Door,* page 57) to the class, or ask one of the children to read it. Discuss the following questions:

1. What is a worrywart?
2. What did Emily worry about when a friend asked her to play and she didn't want to?
3. What else does Emily worry about?
4. What are some things you worry about? (List on the board.)
5. Can you change any of these things yourself? (Make the point that there are some things we worry about that we can do something about. Other things we worry about we cannot change. Encourage the children to do something about the things they can change and to stop worrying about the things they can't.)

Activity: Make a "Good-Bye to Worry" poster. Ask children to trace a hand onto a piece of white construction paper. On the palm, they write "Good-Bye to Worry," and on the fingers, they write things they want to stop worrying about. (Younger children may have trouble writing in the small space created by their traced hands. You could ask them to trace your hand or distribute sheets with a large hand photocopied on them.)

As a second activity, have children make up their own "Worrywart Pledge of Allegiance."

Example:

Some things I can't change,
And some things I can.
When I don't worry,
I give ME a hand!

Worry Dolls

Materials:

- Popsicle sticks OR (for smaller, less elaborate dolls) cotton swabs with wooden sticks for firm control—not plastic or paper shafts
- Fine-tip markers
- Glue
- Pieces of fabric, yarn, ribbon, and construction paper
- Scissors

Pre-activity: Read "The Worry Dolls" (*The Cat at the Door,* page 11). If you have any worry dolls, display them. Lead a discussion based on the following points:

1. One way to cope is to "unload" your problems; you can do this with a friend or a trusted adult, or in prayer.
2. You can even let go of worries by just deciding to shelve them for a while. That's what happens with the worry dolls. You decide to not think about a problem for a while.
3. Ask the children if they've ever let go of a problem at night and awakened thinking of a solution. Encourage them to recount their stories.

Activity: Dispense materials and help the children create little dolls. Eyes and a mouth can be drawn on the cotton top of the swab or one end of the Popsicle stick with a very fine marker. For clothing, just wrap ribbon around the stick, or glue a simple skirt onto the body. *Keep it simple!* The Popsicle stick dolls can be more elaborate, using yarn for hair and fabric or paper for clothes.

Afterward, discuss how the children can tell their worry dolls about their problems, just as they might write their worries in a diary. Discuss some good places to keep their worry dolls: a special box, their school desk, a coin purse.

Wastebasket Ball

Materials:

- Wastebasket
- Paper and pencils or pens

Pre-activity: Read, or ask a child to read, "An Angry Day" (*The Cat at the Door,* page 139). Discuss these questions:

1. Have you ever had a day like Clay's?
2. Did it ever get better? If so, did you notice what happened when you suddenly stopped having a bad day?
3. Ask the children for synonyms and examples of letting go. (Examples: to *lighten up* is to deliberately let go of intense feelings; to *take a break* means to let go of work for awhile and relax; to *forgive* is to let go of angry thoughts and feelings about someone who may have hurt us.)

Activity: Tell the children that today they are going to learn a very physical way of letting go. Distribute the paper, and ask the children to write down the little things that have been bothering them—worries they want to let go of but feel they can't. Encourage the children to write as many things as they want; emphasize that no one will look at their lists but themselves.

Ask the children to wad up their lists. Put an empty wastebasket in the middle of the room, or bring it outside on the playground. The children then get to "throw" their problems away into the wastebasket. You go first, telling everyone to ham it up. This way, the kids get into the physical activity of the game; they are literally letting go of their worries, not just throwing away pieces of paper.

At a moment when the children are really laughing and relaxed, remind them that just moments ago they were scrunched up worrying about things. Drive home the point that games and exercise are excellent ways to let go.

Editorial Note: Sometime before or after the game, the point should be made that of course all problems can't just be thrown away—that if a worry continues to persist, we should try talking about it with someone we trust, such as a parent, friend, counselor, teacher, scout leader, aunt, or uncle. But this lesson emphasizes that letting go of worries—even if just for a few moments—clears our minds and makes us feel better.

Fishing for Good Thoughts
(A Two-Day Activity)

Materials:

- A fish pattern handout (page 51) for each child
- Dowel or stick
- Magnet
- Paper clips
- String
- Glue
- Small strips of paper

Day 1

Pre-activity: Read "A Fish Story" (*The Cat at the Door,* page 90) to the children, or ask one of them to read it to the class.

Tell the class that tomorrow they will play the Fishing For Good Thoughts game. On the board, list some good thoughts that children could say about themselves, and invite the children to add some of their own. (Examples: *I am confident. I make smart choices.*)

Activity: Give each student a fish pattern to color and cut out. Children should tape a paper clip on the inside of one side of the fish and then glue the two sides of the fish together, leaving a small opening at the top for a positive thought strip to fit in. On a small strip of paper, the students write a positive thought.

While the students make the fish, prepare a fishing pole using the dowel or stick and the string. Tie one end of the string to the pole, and glue a heavy magnet to the other end of the string. When the glue on the fish is dry, insert one strip into the top of each fish.

Day 2

Activity: Ask the children to sit in a circle. Pile the fish in the middle of the circle and let the children take turns using the pole to catch a fish. Each child reads the good thought in the fish he or she "catches.

A Friendship Booklet

Materials:

- A copy of the friendship booklet (pages 53-54) for each child
- Crayons or markers
- Scissors
- Staplers for students to share
- Construction paper

Pre-activity: Read "Celebrating with Our Friends" (*The Cat at the Door,* page 106) to the class, or ask one of the students to read it. Discuss the following questions:

1. Why is Claire pleased to go see her friend Brian?
2. How is Claire supportive of her friend?
3. How do you feel when your friends get recognized for special accomplishments?
4. Tell about some things that you do that show you are a good friend.

Activity: Give each child the friendship booklet handout to color. On the last page of the booklet, students write ideas that could help them be good friends. Students cut out each page, make a cover and a back out of construction paper, and staple the booklet together in the upper left corner.

Good friends share.

Good friends care.

To have good friends I must be a good friend.

Ways I Am a Good Friend

Good friends are happy for their friends.

The Friendship Garden

Materials:

- A coloring sheet handout (page 56) for each child
- Crayons or markers

Pre-activity: Read "What You Water Grows" (*The Cat at the Door,* page 82) to the children, or ask one of them to read it to the class. Discuss the following questions:

1. Have you ever had a flower or vegetable garden?
2. What kinds of things are needed to make flowers or vegetables grow?
3. The lesson Kay learns about flowers applies to others things as well. What does she learn? How does this relate to other things in our lives, such as developing good friendships?
4. If we were growing a friendship garden, what would we plant in it? (Examples: love, kindness, joy, happiness, fun, sharing, caring.)

Activity: Distribute copies of the friendship garden coloring sheet. Ask the children to list in the center of each flower something that would help a friendship garden grow. Children may add more scenery before they color their gardens.

Follow-up: Ask for volunteers to show their pictures to the class and tell their classmates what they have in their friendship gardens.

A Friendship Garden

Hand Puppet Express

Materials:

- A hand puppet pattern (page 58) for each child
- Scissors
- Crayons or markers
- Notebook paper
- Glue

Pre-activity: Read "Unpleasant Chores" (*The Cat at the Door,* page 93) to the class, or ask one of the children to read it. Discuss the following questions:

1. Why does Jeff complain about cleaning the bathroom?
2. What important point does Jeff's dad make to him?
3. How does Jeff get in a better mood about doing his chores?

Discuss the idea that how we think, talk, and act about chores can affect whether we have a pleasant experience or an unpleasant experience while doing them.

Activity: Give each child a puppet handout. Tell the children to draw a pleasant expression on one face and an unpleasant expression on the other.

Divide the class into small groups and assign each group a chore topic. Each group is to make up things a person could think, say, and do to create a pleasant experience while doing the task, and things a person could think, say, and do to create an unpleasant experience while doing the task.

Some examples of chores include cleaning your room, doing homework, raking the yard, making your bed, doing the dishes, taking out the garbage, cleaning the cat litter box, vacuuming, and trying on clothes to give away.

After the groups come up with their "think-say-and-do" lists, they read either their pleasant or unpleasant list to the rest of the class. After each list is read, ask "Is this pleasant or unpleasant?" The children hold up their puppets with the expression that matches the experience and call out "Pleasant!" or "Unpleasant!"

On one side draw an unpleasant face. On the other side, draw a pleasant face. Cut out, including circles for fingers. Glue edges together with faces outside.

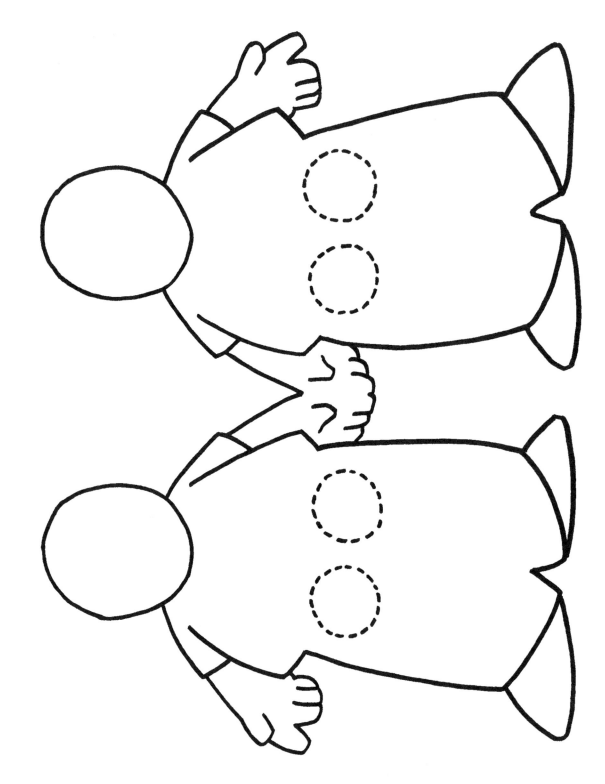

The Get-Over-It Box

Materials:

- A copy of the handout (page 60) for each child
- Shoe box for each child
- Construction paper
- Magazines
- Scissors
- Markers or crayons
- Glue

Pre-activity: Read "The Get-Over-It Box" (*The Cat at the Door*, page 148) to the class, or ask one of the children to read it. Discuss the following questions:

1. What kind of box does Chandra decorate? How does she use her get-over-it box?
2. What kinds of ideas does Chandra put in her get-over-it box?
3. How does this help her?

On the blackboard, write the heading "Getting Over It." Then list the ideas that Chandra puts in her box. Ask the children to suggest more ideas that would be good to get over. Write these on the board too. Then explain how letting go of negative ideas is helpful.

Activity: Cut a slit in the top of each shoe box. Ask the children to decorate it with construction paper. With a marker or crayons, the children should write "My Get-Over-It Box" on the top. Tell the children to decorate the sides of their boxes with pictures from magazines. Distribute the handout to the children. Ask them to fill out the forms and then put them in their get-over-it-boxes.

Something I want to get over: _____

_____

I put this in my get-over-it box and let it go. I agree to think more about solutions than about problems.

Something I want to get over: _____

_____

I put this in my get-over-it box and let it go. I agree to think more about solutions than about problems.

Something I want to get over: _____

_____

I put this in my get-over-it box and let it go. I agree to think more about solutions than about problems.

Something I want to get over: _____

_____

I put this in my get-over-it box and let it go. I agree to think more about solutions than about problems.

Happy Faces

Materials:

- A copy of the "Focusing on Something Good" worksheet (page 62) for each child
- Pencils

Pre-activity: Read "Focusing on Something Good" (*The Cat at the Door,* page 135) to the children, or ask one of the children to read it to the class. Discuss the following questions:

1. What does Abby criticize herself for?
2. What does Abby's friend Nancy tell her?
3. Think of something you criticize yourself about. How do you feel when you criticize yourself? Does criticizing help you change the thing you don't like about yourself?

Activity: Ask the students to read the sentences on the handout. Tell them to draw a happy face beside the affirmations that help them focus on something good about themselves and an unhappy face beside the sentences that focus on negative things.

Focusing on Something Good

Draw a happy face beside the affirmations that help you focus on good things about yourself. Draw an unhappy face beside the sentences that encourage you to think negative things about yourself.

1. I'm really dumb. I will never learn to spell.   _____

2. I treat myself kindly when I make mistakes.   _____

3. I say nice things to myself.   _____

4. Smiling helps me feel good.   _____

5. I don't have any friends.   _____

6. I do a lot of stupid things.   _____

Ability Affirmations

Materials:

- Notecards
- Pencils
- Paper
- Dice, one pair for each group of children

Preparation: For each group of students, write twelve age-appropriate abilities or talents on separate notecards (suggestions: playing a musical instrument, fishing, writing stories, dancing, painting, spelling, playing sports). Choose talents that are common among the children you work with. Turn the cards over and number them one through twelve.

Pre-activity: Read "No Comparison" (*The Cat at the Door*, page 46) to the class, or ask one of the students to read it. Ask, *Why does it bother Keith when he's told that his brother Jason is a "hard act to follow"? What does Keith do when he decides he doesn't have to follow in Jason's footsteps? What does it mean to "accept yourself for what you are"?*

Activity: Ask the children to list on a piece of paper talents and abilities that they have developed and those they would like to develop. These may all go on the same list. Invite the children to share items they have on their lists. List these on the board. In discussion, point out how different children have different abilities.

Tell the class that they are going to play an affirmation game to help them improve their talents or abilities.

Divide the class into groups of no more than six. Give each group a pair of dice and a set of the notecards you prepared. Children roll the dice and select the card that matches the number they roll. They read the talent or ability on the card and make up an affirmation that would help them develop that talent or ability.

Variation: Instead of preparing the cards yourself, ask the children to help you, using the blackboard list of abilities generated by the children.

Creativity Basket

Materials:

- Basket
- Numerous household or office supplies and knickknacks (Post-It notes, paper clips, Fun Foam pieces, ribbons, rubber bands, toilet paper rolls, toothpaste boxes, cotton swabs, pieces of cardboard). There should be *two* of each item, and *only* enough items for each child in the class to pick one (so that each child can pair up for the activity).

Pre-activity: Read "More Solutions Than You Can Dream Of" (*The Cat at the Door,* page 70) or "'Paws' for Creativity" (*The Cat at the Door,* page 133).

Activity: Place all the items in the basket. Each child picks an item from the basket and has five minutes to think of all the possible things that could be done with it. After that period, each child is matched up with the other child who picked the same item. Each pair of children then compares lists. They create a new list of combined items and try to come up with more items.

Children then present their lists to the class. Through discussion, help the children understand the following concepts:

- The mind is incredibly creative; given a problem and time, we can come up with many ideas.
- When two or more people work together, they can come up with more ideas than either could while working alone.
- Though this exercise seems trivial, the skills of thinking creatively and brainstorming can be applied to very big problems, such as pollution and the environment.

Variation: Ask each child to bring in a matching pair of small objects to go in the creativity basket.

Affirmation Guessing Game

Materials:

- Index cards
- Pencils
- Chalkboard and chalk OR flip chart and markers

Pre-activity: Read "Asking For What You Want" (*The Cat at the Door,* page 71), or ask one of the children to read it to the class. Discuss the following questions:

1. What does Terry tell his mom about learning to say what he wants?
2. Are there some things you have a hard time asking for?
3. Why is it important to be able to ask for what you want?

Activity: Give all the children an index card. Ask them to print a brief affirmation on the card and underline each letter in the affirmation. Call on one child to come to the board to draw blank spaces representing each letter of his or her affirmation, making a slash between each word. Ask the child to draw a large circle beside the affirmation. Check to make sure the correct number of blank spaces is written on the board.

Children raise their hands and guess letters to go in the blank spaces. The child at the board writes in the letters when they are guessed correctly. If a letter that is not in the affirmation is guessed, the child lists it in the circle.

The child who correctly guesses the affirmation gets to go to the board next and write the blank spaces for his or her affirmation.

Laughter Mosaic

Materials:

- A copy of the mosaic pattern (page 67) for each child
- Crayons or markers
- Joke book
- Tape recorder

Pre-activity: Read "Laughitis" (*The Cat at the Door,* page 37) to the class, or ask one of the students to read it. Discuss the following questions:

1. Rainbow tells her mom that Debbie is contagious. What has Rainbow caught from her friend?
2. Do you like to laugh?
3. Is laughing good for you? (Yes. It makes us feel good inside and out. It relieves tension and helps us be less serious.)

Activity 1: Give each child a mosaic handout. Ask the children to color the letters with dots in them all the same color to find the happy thought. Then they can color in the other shapes to make a mosaic design. Hang the mosaics on the bulletin board.

Activity 2: Have a "laugh session." Read some jokes to your class to get them in a laughing mood. Then make a "laugh tape" by asking your class to see how long they can laugh. Play the tape back to your class whenever you want to have fun.

Color each letter that has a dot on it with the same color to find the happy thought. Color the rest of the shapes with different colors. Cut out and use for a bulletin board.

Using Good Humor

Materials:

- Paper
- Pencils

Pre-activity: Read "Laugh Lines" (*The Cat at the Door,* page 137) to the class, or ask one of the students to read it. Discuss the following questions:

1. What are some things that Anne adores about Nancy?
2. What does Nancy like about Anne?
3. What does it mean to have a good sense of humor?

Activity: Tell the class they are going to have a few minutes to write down as many funny things as they can think of. They can list things they've heard, seen, or done that made them laugh. Ask some of the students to share what they wrote down.

Follow-up: After the children share, read "Practical Jokes" (*The Cat at the Door,* page 40) to the class, or ask one of the students to read it. Discuss the following questions:

1. What is the joke Jim plays on Sherry and Ned?
2. What does it mean to play a joke at someone else's expense?
3. What can you do to help you decide whether or not a joke you want to play is hurtful to someone? (You may use this question to reinforce the Golden Rule: Treat others as you would like to be treated.)

Refrigerator Magnets

Materials:

- Refrigerator magnet designs (page 70), copied on card stock paper, for each student (Professional copy stores have this stock paper and can make the copies.)
- Markers or crayons
- Glue
- Magnetic tape cut in 1/2-inch strips
- Scissors

Pre-activity: Read "Making A Sandwich" (*The Cat at the Door*, page 81) to the children, or ask one of them to read it. Discuss the following questions:

1. What does making a sandwich usually mean?
2. The Bradford family makes a different kind of sandwich. Give the recipe for the sandwich they make.
3. What are the Bradfords expressing when they make this special sandwich?
4. What are some things your family does to show love?

Activity: Give each child a sheet of refrigerator magnet designs. Children color and cut out each decoratively framed affirmation and glue a small piece of magnetic tape on the back. Children can place these on refrigerators, metal lockers, or any metal surfaces.

Follow-up: Suggest that whenever the children see their magnets hanging up, they repeat the affirmations to themselves.

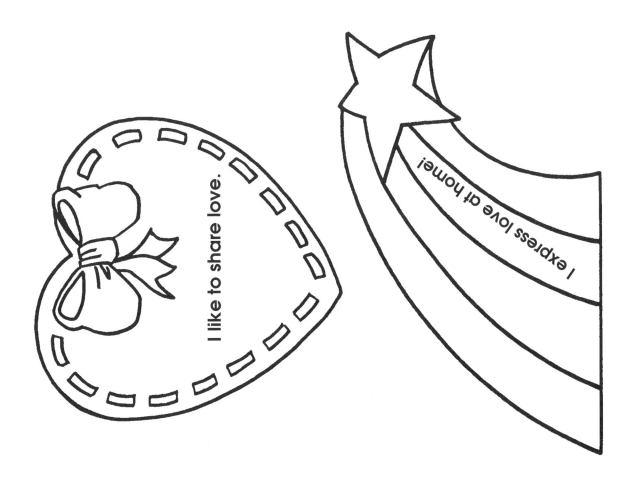

I like to share love.

I express love at home!

I am thankful for my home.

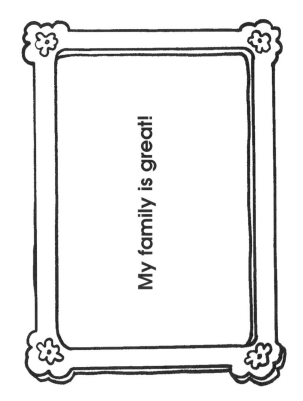

My family is great!

Scarecrow

Materials:

- A copy of the scarecrow and bird handout (page 72) for each child
- Construction paper
- Markers or crayons
- Scissors
- Glue

Pre-activity: Read "Scarecrow" (*The Cat at the Door,* page 48) to the children, or ask one of them to read it to the class. Discuss the following questions:

1. Why do Maryanne, Dick, and their dad build a scarecrow in the garden?
2. How is a mind like a garden?
3. What keeps good ideas from growing in the garden of the mind?
4. How could you be your own scarecrow?

Activity: Give each child a handout of the scarecrow and birds. Tell the children to color and cut out the scarecrow, then write negative phrases on the crows. (Suggest phrases you hear your students use, such as "Dumb idea!" "You always mess up!" or "You can't do that!") Then they draw a garden of plants on the construction paper. They color and cut out the pictures on the handout and paste them on their garden scene.

The Sky's the Limit

Materials:

- Blue construction paper
- Manila or white paper
- Pencils
- Glue

Pre-activity: Read "The First-Day-of-School Blues" (*The Cat at the Door,* page 117) or ask one of the children to read it. Discuss the following questions:

1. What are some of the things that make Angela nervous on her first day at school?
2. What are some things that have happened at school that upset you? What are some ideas you have had about school that make you feel nervous?
3. What does Angela discover when she writes her thoughts about school on the clouds?
4. Name some things you like about school. (Examples: *I like to read. My friends are in my class. Learning is fun. Math is interesting.*)

Activity: Direct the children to tear out cloud shapes from white or manila construction paper and write positive thoughts about school on each cloud. They then make posters by gluing the clouds onto the blue paper. Tell them to label their posters "Good Thoughts About School."

Variation: This can also be used for a bulletin board. Cover the board with blue paper. Give each child a sheet of white construction paper. Ask the children to tear out one large cloud shape and write a good idea about school on it. A good title for the bulletin board is "The Sky's the Limit in School."

Thank-You Cards

Materials:

- A copy of the thank-you card handout (page 75) for each child
- Crayons, markers, or colored pencils

Pre-activity: Read "Thank You" (*The Cat at the Door,* page 163) to the children, or ask one of them to read it. Discuss the following questions:

1. Mr. Watts asks the class to tell him something they like people to say to them. The whole class nods in agreement to Margie's reply. What is her reply?
2. Mr. Watts makes some good suggestions to the children. What are his suggestions?
3. What are you thankful for?
4. What do you do to show appreciation for the good things in your life?

Activity: Give each child a thank-you card handout. Students color the design on the thank-you card, then fold the card in half horizontally, so that the design is on the outside, and then again vertically. On the inside of the card, they write a special note of appreciation to a parent, friend, principal, teacher, special speaker, or another class. Use this activity anytime you have a need for thank-yous in your class.

(FOLD)

(FOLD)

Thumbs-Up Thoughts

Materials:

- A copy of the handout (pages 77 and 78) for each child
- Four ink pads (washable!)
- Pens

Pre-activity: Read "The Sponge" (*The Cat at the Door,* page 142) to the class, or ask one of the children to read it. Discuss the story, focusing on the following questions:

1. How are human minds similar to and different from sponges?
2. Can people choose what they let their minds absorb?
3. What kinds of things does Andrew tell himself when someone says something unkind to him?
4. What does Andrew do at night before he goes to sleep?

Lead a discussion about the kinds of thoughts that are good for people to let into their minds. These are thoughts that help people develop good attitudes and feel good about themselves. The thoughts that are good to discard are those that make people feel bad or downgrade themselves. A way to label thoughts is to call them "thumbs-up thoughts" or "thumbs-down thoughts." The thumbs-up thoughts are the ones that are good for our minds. The thumbs-down thoughts are good to discard.

Activity: Children will do this activity individually. Each child reads the statements on the handout and decides which statements are thumbs-up thoughts and which are thumbs-down thoughts. Children ink their thumbs and put a "thumbs-up" or a "thumbs-down" mark at the end of the statement on the line provided. (Use washable ink or tell the children to draw a thumbs-up or a thumbs-down.)

Variation: Read the statements out loud to the class. Tell the students to hold their thumbs up or down according to the type of thought it is. They can also call out "Thumbs up!" or "Thumbs down!" at the appropriate time.

Thumbs-Up and Thumbs-Down Thoughts

Read each thought and decide which ones are good for your mind. Use thumbs up for the good thoughts and thumbs down for the bad thoughts.

I like me.   _____

Making mistakes is natural. I can learn
from my mistakes.   _____

I'm not good at anything.   _____

Life stinks.   _____

I have a lot of friends in my life.   _____

I don't like change. New experiences
always scare me.   _____

I love life.   _____

Thumbs-Up and Thumbs-Down Thoughts

I like sharing with my friends.   _____

I hate to get up in the morning.   _____

School is boring.   _____

Doing chores is totally gross.   _____

Life is fun. I'm glad to be alive.   _____

I appreciate good things people

do for me.   _____

What I Am

Materials:

- Manila paper
- Markers
- Blackboard and chalk

Pre-activity: Read "What I Am" (*The Cat at the Door,* page 110) to the class, or ask one of the children to read it aloud. Discuss the following questions:

1. How does Anita describe herself with her collage?
2. How does Deborah describe herself?
3. What are some good words that describe what you are like and what things you do?

Activity 1: Write "I Am" in large letters across the blackboard. Choose a student to write his or her name vertically down the side of the board. Ask the class to call out positive words that begin with the letters in the student's name. The student at the board writes the words next to the letters of his or her name. This activity can be done over several days until each student gets a turn.

Activity 2: Students make individual posters. Tell the children to write "I Am" across the top of their posters and to write their name down the side. Next to each letter of their name, they write positive words that begin with the same letter. Then they decorate their special posters.

Life Balance

Materials:

- Old magazines (one per child)
- Scissors
- Glue
- Poster board or construction paper

Pre-activity: Read "Alone Time" (*The Cat at the Door,* page 128) or "Soccer-Crazy" (*The Cat at the Door,* page 146) or ask a child to read one of them to the class. Ask the children to describe the problem in the story. (In "Alone Time," the children don't have any time for themselves. In "Soccer-Crazy," Brent spends all of his time doing one thing—playing soccer—and hurts his social life.)

Write the word *balance* on the chalkboard and say that it is the focus of the stories and today's activity. Using the analogy of a person balancing on a tightrope—he or she cannot lean too far in either direction without falling—explain that balance is ordering our lives so that we do not do too much of one thing or one kind of thing. And like a tightrope walker, when we are out of balance we feel nervous.

On the blackboard, list the following five categories, which depict activities of daily life:

1. Hygiene and daily health care (taking a bath, flossing, eating, sleeping, fixing hair)
2. Sports and activities after school (dance, karate, piano)
3. Private, unstructured time (writing in a dairy, reading, talking on the phone with friends, watching TV)
4. Work or chores around the house
5. School time (homework and related school activities, such as selling wrapping paper for the PTO, practicing for band, and riding the bus)

Activity: Give each child an old magazine and a piece of construction paper or poster board. The children go through their magazines to cut out depictions of activities that fit into these five categories.

Children paste their pictures onto the construction paper or poster and entitle them "A Balanced Life" or a similar title.

The "I Can Balance My Life" Workbook

Materials:

- Workbook handout (pages 82-84) for each child
- Crayons or markers
- Stapler
- Scissors

Pre-activity: Do the "Life Balance" exercise (page 80).

Activity: Distribute the workbook handouts. Ask the children to color and fill out the appropriate lists on page 4 in the handout. Staple the booklets together. Either let the children take their workbooks home to show their parents, or save the booklets to discuss at a meeting with the parents.

I Can Balance My Life

_____

My Name

↓

_____

If all I did was play team sports
Would there be time to build neat forts?
To talk with friends or play my sax?
Pet my cat, or learn math facts?

1

If all I did was fix my hair
Would there be any time to spare
for playing and talking and walking the dog
Or would I just be in a hair-spray fog?

2

No doubt about it, I can see
It's important just to be.
There's always lots of things to do
Balancing them is the clue.

3

1. Health Care

2. Sports/Lessons

3. Work/Chores

4. School/Homework

Here are four lists that describe my day:
Work and health and sports and play.

4

-----

5. Alone Time

But there's a fifth thing: it's time for ME!
When I can discover what it means just to be.
I'm not being lazy or boring, at all
when I go to my room to get away from it all!

5

Notes

Notes

Notes

Other titles that will interest you...

The Cat at the Door and Other Stories to Live By
Affirmations for Children
   by Anne D. Mather and Louise B. Weldon, illustrated by Lyn Martin
   These 183 one-page stories focus on common childhood events and end with a positive message that nurtures a child's sense of self. For grades K through 6, 192 pp.
Order No. 5131

Families in Transition
A Cross-Curricular Guide to The Maple Street Kids
   by Pamela Olson
   A practical, hands-on resource that includes cross-curricular activities and reproducible worksheets to help promote students' self-esteem skills. For grades 3 through 6, 72 pp.
Order No. 1473

Inside Out Workbooks
   by Gretchen Van Kleef Douthit
   These subject-focused workbooks help young people understand their feelings, develop good relationships and self-esteem, and achieve their goals. Includes brief topic introductions followed by open-ended questions for children to complete. Reproducible. For grades 5 and up, 28 pp. each.

My Family and Friends
Order No. 5557

My Goals
Order No. 5556

My Feelings
Order No. 5559

A collection of all 4 workbooks
Order No. 0860

My Self-Esteem
Order No. 5558

**For price and order information, or a free catalog,
please call our Telephone Representatives.**

HAZELDEN EDUCATIONAL MATERIALS

1-800-328-9000
(Toll Free. U.S., Canada & the Virgin Islands)

1-612-257-4010
(Outside the U.S. & Canada)

1-612-257-1331
(FAX)

Pleasant Valley Road • P.O. Box 176 • Center City, MN 55012-0176

Hazelden Europe
PO Box 616 • Cork, Ireland
Telephone: Int'l Access Code+353-21-314318
FAX: Int'l Access Code+353-21-961269